Conte

Introdu

Captain's Commands

Introduction

Welcome to the second volume of Pocket Playground Games. This handy little book contains twenty-three traditional and new playground games.

Playground games provide the ideal opportunity to engage children in enjoyable activities together, promoting positive relationships between the children themselves and the children and adults. Playground games also encourage valuable social skills such as:

- Turn-taking
- Developing speaking and listening skills
- Developing a positive attitude to participation
- Learning to abide by rules
- Interacting with others
- Cooperating
- Having fun

Playground games also encourage energetic exercise, an important aspect that is often neglected in today's hi-tech society and that is an essential part of physical well-being.

The games included in this booklet are set out in a clear, accessible style with easy-to- follow instructions. Playground games provide an ideal occupation for free time that can motivate all children to be part of a group. They will enhance playground experiences for the children involved, create a positive dynamic and generate much fun and enjoyment for all.

Captain's Commands

1. The players stand in the middle of the playground and one is chosen to be the captain.

2. The commands are explained to the players as follows:

(The last player to reach the designated area for the first four commands is out.)

Bow – everyone races to one end of the playground (the front of the boat).

Stern – everyone races to the opposite end of the playground (the back of the boat).

Starboard – everyone races to the right hand side of the playground.

Port – everyone races to the left hand side of the playground.

Man the lifeboats – players get into groups of four. Anyone not in a group is out.

Man o'War approaching – everyone freezes. Anyone who moves is out.

Captain's inspection – all players form a straight line and stand tall; the last player to get in line is out.

3. The captain calls out a command and all the players race to the designated area or comply with the command. When all players have completed the command, any player who is out sits on the sidelines.

4. The captain calls a new command.

5. The captain can be changed at any time and the game begins again with all players back in the middle.

Who Stole the Cookies from the Cookie Jar?

1. Everybody stands or sits in a circle.

2. They all clap their knees and hands once and chant, **'Who stole the cookies from the cookie jar?'**

3. A chosen player calls out another player's name; **'Mary'**, for example.

4. Everybody claps and chants, **'Mary stole the cookies from the cookie jar.'**

5. Then Mary claps and says, **'Who me?'**

6. The other players clap and say, **'Yes, you.'**

7. Mary claps her hands and says, **'Couldn't be.'**

8. Everybody claps and says, **'Then who?'.**

9. Mary claps and calls out another name; for example, **'Ben'**

10. Everyone claps their hands and says: **'Ben stole the cookies from the cookie jar.'**

11. The game continues as before.

Gorilla Game

1. All the players stand in a circle.

2. Each player puts their left hand, palm up, underneath the right hand of the player to their left.

3. Then they place their right hand, palm up, on top of the left hand of the player to their right.

4. Choose a player to start and they pretend to have gorilla snot in their right hand and pass it to the player on their left, who then passes it to the player on their left and so on.

5. While the 'gorilla snot' is being passed around the players sing:

'Down in the jungle, where nobody goes, there's a great big gorilla, picking his nose... and he's picking it ... (repeat four times) **... Whose gonna get that** (repeat three times) **... SLIMEY SNOT!'**

6. The player has the 'gorilla snot' at the end of the song is out.

7. Continue playing until there is one player left who is the winner.

Cops and Robbers

1. Choose a playground feature to be a safe base and another area to be the jail.

2. Choose four players to be the cops. The remaining players are robbers.

3. The cops turn to face a wall and close their eyes.

4. They count up to a designated number e.g. twenty, during which the robbers find places to hide.

5. After the count, the cops spread out and try to find and tag the robbers.

6. The robbers try to reach the safe base without being tagged by a cop and can leave their hiding place before being found if they so wish.

7. Any player who is tagged must go the jail and remain there for the duration of the game.

8. Allow the cops three turns to close their eyes, count and search before choosing new cops.

Mr/Mrs Mouse

1. A player is chosen to be Mr or Mrs Mouse.

2. They stand at one end of the playground with their back towards the other players.

3. The other players stand at the opposite end.

4. They call out, **'Mr/Mrs Mouse, can we visit you in your house.'**

5. Mr/Mr Mouse responds with a category e.g. 'If you have an R in your name,' 'If you have a pet dog,' 'if your birthday is in June,' 'If you had toast for breakfast.'

6. Any player who fits into the category called can take one step forward.

7. The first player to reach the end becomes the new Mr/Mrs Mouse.

Fours

1. A player is chosen to be the caller. They stand with their back to the remaining players.

2. The remaining players mingle – they must keep walking around and not stand in groups.

3. The player calls out a number between two and four and the other players must quickly form groups of the number called.

4. Any player not in a group of the correct number is out and must sit on the sidelines for the duration of the game.

5. The players mingle again and the caller shouts out a different number.

6. The game continues until the number of players is too few to make it viable or you decide to change the caller.

Solar System

1. The players stand in a large inward-facing circle.

2. They are named: Venus, Mars, Jupiter and Saturn consecutively around the circle.

3. Call out the name of one of the planets.

4. The players in the named category leave their places and run round the outside of the circle in an anti-clockwise direction back to their places again.

5. The last player to return to the circle is out and sits on the sidelines for the duration of the game.

6. Repeat the process naming different planets and continue calling the planets randomly until there are too few players to make the game viable.

7. If you want to, you can call out two planets at the same time and the players in both categories will run round the circle.

Caterpillar Race

1. Put the players into groups of three or four, depending on age and ability.

2. The players in each group stand in a line, one behind the other.

3. The back three players hold on to the player directly in front of them, either by grasping them around the waist or putting a hand on their shoulder.

4. They practise walking together with right and left legs moving in unison. The front player can call **'Right, left'** if it helps.

5. When the players have mastered walking in this way, line up the 'caterpillars' for a race.

SPLAT!

1. The more the merrier for this game (minimum of six) and all the players form a Circle with one person standing in the middle – the 'Splat Master'.

2. 'Splat Master' points any person in the circle and shouts **'SPLAT'!** That person then has to duck, while the people either side have to 'splat' each other. You have to shout **'SPLAT'** and put the correct hand up (if the person on your left was pointed to and ducked, you have to put out your left hand with palm facing towards the person on the left. Opposite applies for your right).

3. If you're too late with your **'SPLAT'**, then you're out. If you shout **'SPLAT'** at the wrong time, or at the wrong person, then you're out.

4. When someone is out, they sit down wherever they were standing and the circle remains the same until there are only eight people left standing; only then can you make a smaller circle.

5. Continue until there are only two people left and they stand back-to-back.

6. The 'Splat Master' then thinks of a word (the 'Splat-Word') and says it out loud. The 'Splat Master' then calls out a variety of words. With every word that isn't the 'Splat-Word', the two people take a step forward.

7. When the 'Splat Master' calls out the 'Splat-Word', the two have to shout **'SPLAT!'** at each other.

8. The person that was quicker to shout **'SPLAT!'** is the winner.

Who Has Got My Golden Egg?

1. You will need a blindfold and a golden egg for this game. The egg can be made from card.

2. The players stand in an inward facing circle with their hands open behind their backs.

3. A player is chosen to stand in the centre of the circle wearing the blindfold.

4. A second player is chosen to walk around the outside of the circle and place an egg into the open hands of one of the players.

5. The player in the centre is turned several times to disorientate them.

6. The player in the centre calls out, **'Who has got my golden egg?'**

7. The player holding the egg disguises their voice and answers, **'I have got your golden egg?'**

8. The player in the centre has three tries to guess the identity of the player holding the egg.

9. Repeat the process with different players.

Who Dares?

1. Three players are chosen to be giants.

2. Each giant is attached by a long rope tied around their waist to a static feature.

3. The giants stand together and dare the other players to come close to them.

4. The giants wait until other players are close and then try to tag them. The other players quickly run to get out of the giants' range.

5. Any player who is tagged must sit on the sidelines for the duration of the game.

6. After a set time, change the giants and repeat the action.

Spin the Arrow

1. Prepare a spinning arrow (or use a plastic bottle).

2. The players stand in a well-spaced circle.

3. Place the arrow (or bottle) in the centre and spin it.

4. When the arrow stops, the players opposite the head and tail of the arrow (or neck and base of the bottle) run round the outside of the circle back to their places.

5. The last player back is out and sits on the sidelines for the duration of the game.

6. Continue the game with repeated spins of the arrow.

Dodge Ball

1. The players form a large circle.

2. Three or four players are chosen to stand in the middle of the circle.

3. The remaining players throw a large soft ball across the circle and try and hit one of the players in the centre.

4. If a player in the centre is touched by a ball, they swap places with someone from the circle.

5. Play continues until all the players in the circle have had a turn to dodge the ball in the centre.

Dodge Ball 2

1. Four to six players are chosen to be ball rollers.

2. The remaining players stand in a designated area that ensures they are standing quite close to each other.

3. The ball rollers position themselves at equal distances round the outside of the players.

4. They roll the ball on the ground at the players (they must not throw the ball).

5. The players jump over the ball, but cannot move from their original positions.

6. The ball rollers roll the ball backwards and forwards through the players.

7. Any player who is touched by the ball is out and must sit on the sidelines for the duration of the game.

Crossing the Line

1. The players are divided into two equal teams and then the teams line up facing each other at opposite ends of the playground and well spaced apart.

2. A line is drawn in chalk, or indicated by a marker on the sideline, approximately 1.5m in front of each team.

3. Team A gets into a huddle and quietly nominates one of their players who will try and cross through the opposing team. Then Team A spreads out into a line again, hold hands and slowly walk towards team B.

4. When Team A reaches the chalk line or marker, they drop hands and the designated player runs forward and tries to get through a space and behind team B without being tagged. If they are successful, team A wins a point.

5. Team B can leave their places once team A's player has started to run forward.

6. Team A returns to their original position and team B repeats the process.

7. Make sure that the teams maintain their spaces between players when they are lining up to give the opposing team a fair chance to cross the line.

8. Encourage the teams to be very secretive about their designated player and not to look at them when they are about to run forward as this will alert the opposition as to their identity. They need to try and keep the element of surprise.

Swapping Places

1. The players stand in a large circle.

2. One player is chosen to stand in the middle wearing a blindfold.

3. On the command **'Swap places',** the players change their position in the circle.

4. The person in the centre raises their arm and points ahead of them saying, **'What's your name?'**

5. The player who is being pointed at replies, **'My name is --------',** giving a false name.

6. The person wearing the blindfold can have three tries to guess the real identity of the speaker and can ask them to repeat their response twice more before guessing.

Lion Attack

1. Create a large circle with ropes or drawn in chalk that represents the water hole.

2. The players stand in a row with eyes closed and you walk behind the line, tapping three players gently on the shoulder.

3. The three players tapped are lions and they must keep their identity secret.

4. All the players mill around in the water hole.

5. On your command, either by blowing a whistle or calling, **'Lions on the prowl',** the three lions roar and begin to tag other players.

6. The other players try to run out of the water hole to safety.

7. The lions must remain in the water hole and cannot tag players once they have left this area.

8 Any player tagged must sit on the sidelines for the duration of the game.

9. Repeat the process choosing three new lions from the players left in the game.

10. Continue to play until there are too few players to make the game viable.

Underneath the Arches

1. Divide the players into two equal teams.

2. Each team stands in a well-spaced circle. The players hold hands and raise their arms to form arches.

3. Each player in turn leaves their place and runs around the circle in and out of the arches and back to their place.

4. Once they are back in position, the next player repeats the process.

5. The first team to have all players complete the run is the winner.

6. The players must go through every arch and if they miss one, they have to go back to their place and start again.

Farmer, Farmer

1. Name the players consecutively: sheep, pig, cow or chicken.

2. A player is chosen to be the farmer and stands to the side.

3. The remaining players chant, **'Farmer, Farmer who's going to market today?'**

4. The farmer calls out one of the animals and all the children in that category run to the end of the playground and back.

5. The first player back becomes the new farmer.

6. Each outgoing farmer takes on the animal identity of their replacement, which may be different to their original animal.

Sticky Toffee

1. One player is chosen to be the chaser.

2. The remaining players stand nearby with one hand on the chaser.

3. The chaser says a list of shopping items, each with a prefix of 'sticky' and the last item being 'sticky toffee', e.g. 'I went to the shop and bought: sticky sweets, sticky socks, sticky juice, sticky cake, sticky jam, sticky toffee'.

4. When the players hear 'sticky toffee' they run away and the chaser pursues them trying to tag as many as possible.

5. A new chaser is chosen and the game repeated.

Race to the Middle

1. Divide the players into two teams and number them from one upwards.

2. Team A stands in a well- spaced line from one onwards.

3. Team B stands facing team A, but their last player is facing the number one of team A and their player number one is facing the last player in team A.

4. The gap between the two teams should be 2.5 - 3 metres.

5. Place an object or marker in the middle of the gap between the two teams.

6. Call a number at random and the two players with that number leave their places and race to the object in the centre.

7. The first player to touch the object scores a point for their team.

8. Continue to call out the numbers randomly.

9. The winning team is the team with the most points at the end of the game.

Pirate Jack

1. The players stand in a large circle.

2. A player is chosen to be Pirate Jack and walk around the outside of the circle while the rest of the players say the following chant:

'Pirate Jack is sailing back, the pirate bold wants his gold and you will walk the plank 1, 2, 3.'

3. On the count of three, the pirate taps the player in front of him and begins to run around the circle.

4. The player who has been tapped chases Pirate Jack and tries to tag him before he reaches the vacant space.

5. The chasing player becomes the new Pirate Jack.

In the Dragon's Maze

1. Choose three children: one to be the dragon, one to be the explorer and one to be the keeper of the maze.

2. Arrange the rest of the children in rows of equal numbers to form the maze. They should all be standing, facing the same way and holding hands along the rows. Any children left over can be additional explorers.

3. Start the game by telling the explorers to make their way along the passageways of the maze.

4. Ask the dragon to chase them and try to capture them.

5. Tell the keeper to shout **'turn'** and stop the game.

6. On the command of **'turn',** the dragon and explorers freeze. The children in each row drop hands and make a quarter turn in a clockwise direction to form a new row.

7. Start the game again.

8. Each time the keeper calls **'turn',** the children in the rows make a quarter turn to the right to change the direction of the rows.

9. Continue the game until all of the explorers are caught or the children are out of breath.

10. Choose different children to play the parts and start again.